# The Renaissance

*THE BEST ONE-HOUR HISTORY*

Robert Freeman

The Best One-Hour History™

Kendall Lane Publishers, Palo Alto, CA

Copyright © 2013, Robert Freeman

ISBN-13: 978-0-9892502-6-9

# Contents

# 1 Introduction

Civilizations are born. Civilizations die. And sometime—very rarely—they go to sleep and then re-awaken. That's what happened to European civilization after the fall of Rome in 476 C.E (Common Era). For almost a thousand years, until around 1400, Europe was in an extended slumber, a hibernation that later writers would call a "Dark Age." When it finally awoke, it did so with a vitality and a creativity that startled the world, that startled even Europeans themselves. It was almost as if the intellectual glories of Greece and Rome had been brought back to life, as if the majesty of the ancient world had been reborn. Indeed, that is what "Renaissance" means: "Rebirth."

This work discusses the astonishing achievements of the Renaissance. It begins with their origins in the breakdown of the medieval order. It discusses the central idea of the Renaissance, Humanism, and how that idea came to be reflected in art, sculpture, architecture, and letters. It looks at the changes that occurred in Europe's core institutions—politics, economics, science, and religion—and how those changes defined the character of the emerging modern world. Finally, it considers the critical questions of why these tectonic changes occurred in Europe and why they occurred at this particular time.

One of the devices we use to clarify our understanding of major periods is to express their essence in as economical a form as possible. So, for example, we said of the Middle Ages, "After the fall, a thousand year darkness." For that is what happened: Rome fell, and a "darkness" enveloped Europe. In the case of the Renaissance, the simplification we have chosen is this: *"Europe awoke by rediscovering its ancient past."* For that is what the Renaissance really was: a rediscovery of the majesty of Europe's classical past, of Greece and Rome.

Yet, while those legacies had so much to impart, so much more emerged as well. That is the mystery (if not the miracle) of the Renaissance: that it was so fertile in reviving an ancient culture; yet so creative in how it changed that culture into the roots of what we now know as the modern world. This is that story.

# 2  Background: The Middle Ages

For most of its thousand-year span, the Middle Ages rested on two foundations: the Catholic Church; and feudalism. Between them, these two institutions provided the political, economic, religious, social, and cultural contexts for almost all of European life. Virtually nothing occurred in Europe that was not channeled by the influence and tempered by the constraints of one or the other of these two immense institutions.

The Catholic Church was the one institution that had survived the fall of Rome. As such, it wielded much of the authority that had inhered in the Roman Empire. It also came with a built-in administrative system that blanketed Europe with hundreds of monasteries, churches and schools, thousands of local clergy, and the only educated class in all of Europe: the priesthood. Most importantly, it possessed a ready-made system of belief—Christianity—that gave meaning and direction to the lives of the people of the Middle Ages, but that at the same time prevented them from learning any other doctrinal system.

Where the Church provided religious and cultural context to the Middle Ages, feudalism provided political and economic foundations. The vacuum created by the fall of the Roman Empire was not filled by any other singular force. Rather, it was filled by thousands of local overlords who gave protection to peasants in exchange for their loyalty and work, and who contended with other overlords for influence and power. This "political atomization" produced thousands of various-sized fiefdoms that dotted the continent. It only started to change when larger political entities began to emerge around 1500.

In addition to its political role, Feudalism provided the economic context of the Middle Ages as well. Local overlords provided birth-to-death jobs and housing in exchange for a significant portion of what the peasants produced. This was not a buy-and-sell relationship, nor was it slavery. It was a form of social contract that defined mutual obligations between lords and peasants. The peasants were called "serfs" and were bound in this contract to their lords, for life. These economic arrangements, centered on the agricultural self-sufficiency of the lord's estate, proved amazingly durable, as witnessed by their almost unchanged survival over a thousand years.

But durable as they were, these two foundations were not indestructible. In 1300, the Catholic Church was the richest, most powerful institution in all of Europe. But that very wealth and power led to overreaching and corruption, and to reprisals by those who resented it. In 1309, for example, the French king kidnapped the pope and moved the papacy from Rome to the French town of Avignon. It stayed there for 70 years in what became known as the "Babylonian Captivity." This was followed by a four-decade long "Great Schism," where three different "popes" claimed authority and battled for Church control.

There was also dissent emerging from within the Church. Jan Hus was a priest in Bohemia, part of what is the modern-day Czech Republic. He decried Church corruption and proposed that it be governed by councils of members, a practice known as "Conciliarism." Hus' ideas posed a threat to centralized Church power so he was murdered after having been promised safe passage to a Church conclave to discuss his beliefs. These various institutional conflicts combined to damage Church prestige and influence, which it would never again regain. Instead, its authority was increasingly challenged by secular princes and kings who coveted Church wealth, but resented its interference into the running of their affairs.

Feudalism, too, was beginning to decay. The Crusades, which lasted from 1100 to 1300, killed off much of Europe's nobility. The Hundred Years War between France and England did the same. The result was that the middle tier of the King-Noble-

Peasant hierarchy that defined feudalism began to wither. Kings filled the vacuum, taking more and more power unto themselves. Stronger kings consolidated their power into "states," with armies and bureaucracies designed to hold and expand that power. The most successful kingdoms (kings' domains) became nation states, the antithesis of the localized fiefdoms of feudalism. Spain, France, and England were the earliest examples.

The economic foundations of feudalism were eroding as well. The Black Plague in the middle of the 1300s wiped out as much as 40% of Europe's population. That made workers scarce, improving their value to landowners, who had to resort to paying money wages to attract skilled labor. This undermined the "bound-for-life" relationship that lay at the heart of serfdom. Also, the longer distance commerce that had begun with the Crusades fostered occasional "fairs," where traders would come to exchange their wares. These evolved into towns, headed by merchants. Neither towns nor merchants had a place in the traditional feudal hierarchy. They would become the inadvertent agents of feudalism's demise.

Expanded trade also led to an expansion in the use of money, especially to replace barter which was the conventional basis of transactions. Money was superior to barter because of its portability, its durability, and its fungibility—its capacity to be used for any exchange. As was the case with workers earning wages, this undermined one of the foundations of the feudal economy. As this occurred, merchants grew still more, eventually rivaling and in some cases surpassing the feudal nobility in status and influence. As they did so, the towns and cities where they lived became an entirely new cultural locus that bore no connection to the traditional landed feudal estate that in many ways had defined the Middle Ages.

In these and other ways, the two institutional foundations of the Middle Ages—the Catholic Church and feudalism—were steadily eroded, causing a great disruption to the cultural uniformity that had stabilized Europe for the prior thousand years.

# 3   The Explosive Awakening

But old patterns don't disappear into a vacuum. They are always replaced by new ones that fill the gap left by the old. The soldiers who fought the Crusades had made their way to the Holy Lands at the eastern end of the Mediterranean via a sea route that went through the cities of northern Italy. That made those cities, including Venice, Florence, and Milan, among the largest and most prosperous in Europe. In the year 1500, three of the four largest cities in Europe were in Italy.

After the Crusades ended, those northern Italian cities continued their relations with the East, importing the spices, silks, jewels, and other treasures that Europe had discovered and desired. This spawned that new class of actors mentioned above—international traders, shippers, merchants, manufacturers, and bankers—who had little connection to the feudal system. They earned fabulous wealth from their enterprises and developed an entirely new cultural ethic.

Instead of the traditional Christian emphasis on the uncertain hereafter, they focused on the demonstrable here-and-now. Instead of eschewing material wealth as Jesus had taught, they coveted it. Rather than cultivating humility, they consciously pursued self-glorification. They sought to enrich their lives with art and architecture, poetry and worldly learning. It was not an accident that it was in northern Italy, in the wealthiest of Europe's cities, that the Renaissance began.

If there was a singular event that set off the Renaissance, it was the fall of Constantinople in 1453. Rome had been the center of the Western Roman Empire. But there had been an Eastern Roman Empire as well, headed by Emperor Constantine and centered in the city that was named for him. It survived Rome's fall and became the Byzantine Empire. It was there that the cultural treasures of Greece had been preserved during Europe's thousand-year "darkness."

Decades before Constantinople actually fell to the Muslims, the priests and artists, academics and philosophers who guarded that legacy began returning to that place their cultural ancestors had fled almost a thousand years before: Italy. They brought with them the intellectual treasures of Europe's classical past. The rediscovery of Greek roots complemented the recently renewed interest in Roman roots that was already underway in Italy. It was that (re)infusion of cultural vitality—both Greek and Roman—that (re)ignited European civilization.

The Renaissance, then, was an effort to reclaim the glories of Europe's ancient past, the intellectual vitality that was Greece and the physical majesty that was Rome. Rather than focusing on God as the Church had taught, Renaissance thinkers decided to focus on man, as the Greeks and Romans had done. They would not dwell on man's limitations and sinful nature as the Church did, but rather on his dignity, his beauty, his worth, and his potential for limitless growth. And their aspirations for man—for themselves—were almost limitless. As Pico della Mirandola, a revivalist of Plato wrote in 1486, "By choosing wisely, man can become as God."

This focus on humans as the central actor in the world became the animating ethic of the Renaissance. It was given an appropriate name, "Humanism." Humanism would repudiate the sterile, indoctrinating monotony of Church-style education and look, instead, at original texts of the classics to decipher the true path to knowledge and virtue. It would emphasize rhetoric and felicity of expression as means to defend and propagate its views. Most importantly, it would find all of these ideals in the glories of the past, in the high point of human achievement that had once burned so brightly but that had fallen and been encrusted under a millennium of ignorance and superstition.

In these ways, the Renaissance was not only revolutionary, it was a cultural civil war. It was a rebellion against medieval-based Church practices and their suffocating monopoly on approved culture. Humanism focused on the moral freedom of the individual and the dignity that such freedom imparted to those courageous enough to take it up. Typically, one of its most enduring aphorisms, "Man can know and will the Good," was reinterpreted from Cicero's ancient dictum, "The true praise of virtue lies in doing good." It was an exquisitely optimistic, even idealistic, philosophy, one that believed in the improvability, perhaps even the perfectability, of the individual human.

Renaissance scholars, beginning with Petrarch, unearthed, translated, learned, and applied ancient texts. They hoped to discover the wisdom that had made Greece and Rome the progenitors and exemplars of European civilization. Humanism captured the imagination of Petrarch's city of Florence and quickly spread through the rest of northern Italy and eventually to all of the learned circles in Europe. It was especially influential in France, the Dutch and Flemish Low Countries, and in England. It affected art, sculpture, architecture, literature, law, theology, indeed, the entire intellectual edifice of European life.

By reviving European understanding of its original character and its respect for those original ideals, Humanism gave renewed life to European culture. In the process, it laid the foundation for still greater revolutions to follow, in governance, religion, economics, and science. In these critical ways, the Renaissance rightly deserves its translated name: rebirth.

# 4 New Perspectives in Arts and Letters

These new ideals of the Renaissance were given expression in a variety of mediums. Among the most visible and enduring were painting, sculpture, architecture, and letters. From these we know the iconic names of the Renaissance: Michelangelo; Leonardo; Raphael; Machiavelli; Erasmus; and Luther.

*[Author's note: It will very helpful if, while reading the section below, the reader can google the works cited in italics. This will help the reader visualize the works and the innovations discussed in the text.]*

## Painting

It is through painting that the Renaissance is most commonly known. Its works mark a definite divergence from the lifeless, formulaic paintings approved by the Church during the Middle Ages. Instead, the themes are increasingly secular and the portrayals lifelike. Not surprisingly (given the source of their inspiration) painters began to venture toward the mythological and pagan. The use of color, emotions, movement, light and shadow, nature, and the portrayal of subjects as individuals and not just as symbols, are striking even to viewers today. In these ways, Renaissance painters created a distinctive break with the past that underscored the Humanist ideal: to dignify man today.

Perhaps the first painter to make a decisive break from established norms was Giotto di Bondone, or Giotto. Though still primitive by the standards of the later Renaissance, his paintings portrayed life-like figures in life-like settings. In *The Lamentation of Christ*, for example, painted around 1310, Giotto used foreshortening, a technique developed by the Greeks to convey depth in human subjects. He also exhibited a rudimentary form of perspective, to convey depth in settings. Gone were the flat, lifeless, colorless, people-as-symbols so characteristic of painting in the Middle Ages. The later Italian art critic Vasari called Giotto's work "a new beginning" for its contrast with everything that had gone before.

If Giotto was the first true Renaissance painter, the first great Renaissance painter was Masaccio. Masaccio blended subject and setting more gracefully than had Giotto, and added more sophistication to the use of emotions and perspective. His *Adam and Eve*, painted, in 1427, portrays three dimensions and contains visual imagery (arches) that harkens back to Rome. It presents Adam and Eve in the nude, a startling departure from the more priggish standards of medieval art, a standard that would be adopted by later great masters including Botticelli and Michelangelo. Masaccio's *Holy Trinity* is a masterpiece in its use of perspective and the technique known as *trompe l'oeil* where the artist "deceives the eye," in this case by creating the illusion of a recess in the wall when it is actually the flat surface of a painting the viewer is seeing.

The work of Sandro Botticelli represents a still further evolution in both the technique and subject matter. Botticelli's most memorable paintings adopt mythological and pagan themes, a sign of the incipient rebellion against the centuries-long domination of art by the Catholic church. His early masterpiece, *Primavera*, completed in 1480, depicts a rite-of-spring celebration between Greek Gods and mortals. It is laden with mythological allusions and symbols. His later masterpiece, *Birth of Venus*, painted in 1486, is also pagan in subject matter and even more arresting in technique. Its central character, Venus, is painted naked and in a startlingly sensual, even voluptuous style. Both paintings are set in nature, a classic Renaissance device, and, again, a symbol of the growing pagan values that came part and parcel with the revival of Greek culture.

The first painter of the "High Renaissance" was Leonardo da Vinci. Leonardo was a prodigious genius, working in painting, anatomy, engineering, design, and other disciplines. Though his output in painting was somewhat meager (only ten of his works still exist today), his influence was extraordinary. His *Last Supper*, completed in 1498, combines virtually all of the techniques of classic Renaissance art: nature, perspective, emotion, movement, color, light, shadow, individuality, and deep religious symbolism. Leonardo's *Mona Lisa*, painted in 1505, may be the single most recognized painting ever created. Leonardo's genius was acknowledged in his own time and he was employed by popes, princes and kings throughout Europe.

Raphael Sanzio, or Raphael, was a contemporary of Leonardo's and another of the towering geniuses of the High Renaissance. He produced a stupendous output encompassing both religious and non-religious subjects alike. His *School of Athens*, painted around 1510, is a paean to the titans of a pagan age: Plato and Aristotle, who are the central subjects. It also heralds Euclid, Pythagoras, Socrates, Ptolemy, and more than a dozen other giants of the secular Greek pantheon. Raphael's *Transfiguration*, completed in 1520, both astounded and awed his contemporaries. It foreshadowed the schools of painting known as Mannerism with its twisted, agonized human forms, and Baroque with its stark contrasts of good and evil.

Michelangelo Buonarotti saw himself as more a sculptor than a painter but his genius made him the last great painter of the High Renaissance. He is best known for his painting of the ceiling of the

*Sistine Chapel* in the Vatican, completed in 1512. The painting, done in fresco, is overwhelming in its scale, scope, and depth. It is explosive with the drama of Biblical narrative, from the creation to the crucifixion. The intricate portrayal of such vast subject matter makes it one of the seminal events in the entire history of art. Michelangelo's *Last Judgment* covers the wall behind the altar of the Sistine Chapel. It was the largest single fresco painting of its century but created huge controversy due to the prevalence of exposed male genitals in a place of such sacred importance.

## Sculpture

If one of the Renaissance's ideals was to portray reality "as it is," then sculpture may have been its most authentic medium. Only through sculpture could the artist portray all three dimensions of space in a single work. One of the earliest sculptors to break from the sterile formulas of medieval orthodoxy was Lorenzo Ghiberti. Ghiberti won an Italy-wide competition in 1401 to create a set of *doors for the Baptistery at the cathedral in Florence.* The competition had attracted entrants from all over Italy. Ghiberti took 20 years to complete the commission and was rewarded with a second set of doors to design and create. The doors, which portrayed scenes from the Old and New Testaments, became icons of their age, attracting sculptors from all over Europe who came to study them.

Great though he was, Ghiberti was surpassed by one of his own students, Donato di Niccolo, or Donatello as he was known. Donatello was to sculpture what Masaccio had been to painting: its first great Renaissance practitioner. His figures convey the emotions and individual faces one sees in real people. His *St. John the Evangelist* uses distorted proportions so that it looks more imposing from the vantage of the viewer, a technique later used by Michelangelo in his monumental *David*. Vasari, a late-Renaissance art critic and biographer, wrote that "there is a wonderful sense of life bursting from the stone" of Donatello's statues. Donatello was one of the first artists to become a living celebrity, a stature reflecting the society's esteem for artists.

Unquestionably, the most famous of Renaissance sculptors was Michelangelo. He completed carving the *Pieta*, a rendering of the dead Jesus in the arms of his mother, Mary, in 1499 when he was only 26 years old. It evokes a pathos that few other works of art in any medium have ever rivalled. Michelangelo's *David*, also completed before his thirtieth birthday, is even more famous, probably the most recognizable statue in the world. It stands over 13 feet tall and is regarded as the near perfect portrayal of both youthful strength and human beauty. Michelangelo's last major work of sculpture was completed in 1515: the 8 foot tall figure of *Moses* holding the Ten Commandments. After Moses, Michelangelo started many other works of sculpture but most were left unfinished. He died fifty years after completing it.

## Architecture

More than any place in Europe, Italy was inescapably conscious of the grandeur of its ancient past. The country was literally a garden of decomposed ruins and still-standing monuments to Roman glory. So, as prosperity returned to northern Italy in the fourteenth century and as its wealthy city-states undertook a vast wave of new construction, partly to commemorate, partly to advertise its recent economic success, the question of a new architectural style begged for definition.

The most influential of the early architects of the Italian Renaissance was Filippo Brunelleschi. His *Cathedral of Florence* is considered one of the first true Renaissance buildings. In classic Renaissance fashion, Brunelleschi used the Pantheon in Rome as the model but contributed several innovations of his own. The dome is much larger and higher than that of the Pantheon and it uses no centering supports. Many early observers of its design doubted that it could actually be built, but when it was completed in 1436 it was an instant success. Brunelleschi used graceful proportions and a simplification of all the parts to create an elegant, harmonious whole. These features—simplification, balance, and proportion— became the essential characteristics of Renaissance architecture.

Successful though he was, Brunelleschi never generated a theory of his work or approach. Leon Batista Alberti took up that challenge and in 1485 wrote what was to become the "Bible" of Renaissance architecture, *De Re Aedificatoria*. In it, Alberti formalized the design system that Bruneleschi had created. He expounded on everything from theory and practice to materials and methods. He discussed religious, civic, and domestic buildings as well as the larger issues of city planning and design. *Aedificatoria* included a specific theory of beauty and function that was rooted in the classics but that still allowed for adaptations to present day needs. Its influence was so great it became impossible for later architects to work without considering its guidance.

Donato Bramante's trademark was the enclosure of vast internal space that inspired wonder in those who entered it. His most famous design is *St. Peter's Cathedral* in Rome, by far the most recognizable Christian church in the world. Its dome rises 450 feet and can be seen for miles from all around the city. The project was so complex it took almost 200 years to complete. It was overseen by 12 different follow-on architects and 30 popes. With so many different hands in the matter, including those of Michelangelo who managed the project while in his eighties, its parentage is sometimes confused. But it was Bramante's design that endured and that came to be built.

## Letters

Though art is its most visible manifestation, the Renaissance really began in the realm of letters, with Francesco Petrarch around 1350. Petrarch was a poet who lived in Florence and who was dissatisfied with the ossified cultural inheritance of his age. It was he who coined the term "Dark Ages" to describe the interval since the fall of Rome. Petrarch declared that scholars would have to return to the original sources of Europe's glory, the writings of the statesmen, poets, and philosophers of ancient Rome. He searched libraries throughout Italy to uncover such documents and began a systematic translation of them. Petrarch's writings influenced virtually all subsequent writers and artists of the Renaissance. He is rightly called, "The Father of the Renaissance."

Renaissance writers were skeptical of much of what were passed off as authoritative documents, especially those that instilled power in the Church. In one of the most incendiary episodes of the analysis of original texts (as Petrarch had advocated), Lorenzo Valla, a Catholic priest, proved that the *Donation of Constantine*, in which Emperor Constantine reposed authority in the Roman Church, was a fraud, written in the 800's instead of in the 300's as the Church had represented. This posed such a threat to the legitimacy of the Church's claim to power that it threatened to have Valla executed. His life was only spared by the intervention of King Alphonso of Naples, Valla's patron.

Pico della Mirandolla wrote a document that, as much as any other, epitomized the optimistic, Humanist ethos of the Renaissance. His *Oration on the Dignity of Man*, completed in 1486, borrows directly from Plato in describing man's place as "half way between the beasts and God." Indeed, God created man last, said Mirandolla, so that man could contemplate all the rest of God's creation and revel in its beauty. In this position, man has the freedom of choice to gravitate toward whatever he chooses to contemplate, whether the beasts or God. It is in this freedom that man finds his essential dignity—but only if he chooses well. Mirandolla's nakedly flattering portrait of man could not be more different from the Church's concept of man as fallen and sinful.

Perhaps the most famous writer of the Renaissance was the Florentine gentleman, Niccolo Machiavelli. His famous essay, *The Prince*, is widely assumed to be a manual for political treachery. In fact, Machiavelli wrote *The Prince* to help educate the ruler of Florence following the invasion of the city by the French king, Charles VIII, in 1494. The essay discusses the rough-and-tumble realities of political survival. It portrays the truth about political machinations, the acquisition of power, the intrigue and ruthlessness required to keep power, and the character of the successful ruler. *The Prince* was revolutionary for the way it put aside the pretense of moral ideals in favor of the reality of secular power. In this way—its preference for reality over ideals—it is the epitome of Renaissance thought. It remains one of the classics of political literature to this day.

At the same time Machiavelli was writing of political realities in Italy, Sir Thomas More was writing of political fantasy in England. His *Utopia* uses an imagined world as a device to criticize political institutions in Tudor England. Rather than "a perfect place," *Utopia*, in fact, means, "no place." It was written in response to More's reading of the voyage of Amerigo Vespucci in the New World. More intended the reader to reflect on the condition of his own society, the better to improve it. In classic Renaissance fashion, *Utopia* was heavily influenced by Plato's *Republic*, where the Greek philosopher laid out the contours of what he believed to be the best form of governance. Its message, "we can do better," echoes the hopeful sentiment that underlaid so much of Renaissance thought.

The great Dutch humanist, Desiderius Erasmus, was a friend if More's. He was a devoted Catholic priest who published a new Bible based on his comparison of original Greek texts with the Latin texts used by the Church. He was able to prove that the Holy Trinity—the Father-Son-Holy Ghost doctrine central to Christian theology—was invented somewhere in the early 300s and was not part of Jesus' teachings. As with Valla's *Donation*, this called into question the authenticity of fundamental Church claims. Erasmus maintained an active correspondence with Martin Luther, but broke with Luther after Luther's condemnation of the Church. It was later written that "Erasmus laid the egg that Luther hatched," a reference both to his stature within European intellectual circles, and to the legitimacy he gave to challenging Church authority.

# 5   New Institutions

The art of the Renaissance was beautiful and the sculpture was inspiring. Its architecture enriched the lives of its people and its humanist philosophy was ennobling. But with the exception of public architecture, these things were almost exclusively the province of a wealthy few. Moreover, the dominant art forms soon morphed into something else and the philosophy mutated as well. Europe moved beyond Greece and Rome as the bases for its ongoing revival.

What endured, however, were the spirit of inquiry, the impetus to challenge authority, and the focus on reality as opposed to theological ideals. These produced institutional changes in the more mundane areas of life, in technology, industry, economics, religion, and politics. Their novelty here was just as great as were the changes in the arts, but they proved more far reaching and enduring. As a result, the changes created in these arenas formed the foundations of the modern world.

## Printing and the Birth of Literacy

The invention of printing in 1455 was one of the most important catalysts of a "new" world. It is impossible to overstate just how momentous the impact of printing really was, both in terms of how it helped spread Renaissance ideas and on the development of other technologies.

In just the fifty years following Gutenberg's invention, over six million books were printed representing over 40,000 different titles. The numbers and range of subjects indicate just how quickly Europe developed a broad class of literate citizens. The new books included titles on law, philosophy, weights and measures (important for trade), medicine, maps (important for exploration), city-building, farming, dictionaries, grammars, and all fields of engineering (important for building rapidly expanding cities). Also printed were books on weapons, hydraulics, shipbuilding and navigation, mining, clock making, astronomy and metallurgy. Finally, new editions included books for leisure and entertainment of the masses—novels, plays, poems, games, and recipe and joke books.

Printing greatly increased the speed at which new knowledge spread while literacy increased the speed at which at which that new knowledtge was absorbed into the culture. Before printing, discoveries typically spread by word of mouth, which was slow, usually one-to-one, and unreliable. With printing, the exact same information could go to thousands of people at the same time, with complete reliability. And almost all of these books were written in the vernacular, in the language of local people, not in Latin, as the Catholic Church had practiced. This meant that new knowledge could be absorbed more quickly.

The result was an astounding outpouring of invention, innovation, citizenship, and wealth that occurred nowhere else in the world. At the time the Renaissance began, Europe was at the same level of economic development as the other major civilizations of the world. By the time it was over, Europe had begun to pull away from the other civilizations, producing knowledge, wealth, and, therefore, power that would not be equaled for many centuries to come.

## Emergence of Centralized (Nation) States

One of the primary features of the Middle Ages was a diffuse feudal nobility that shared power with regional monarchies. But during the Renaissance, in what we now know as Spain, England and France, the balance of power began to shift in favor of the monarchies. The change marked the emergence of centralized states where all people of a single, common language are governed by a single, common ruler. Such "nation states" are the form of government recognized in most of the world today.

In Spain, Ferdinand of Aragon and Isabella of Castile, began the unification of the Spanish crown by their marriage in 1469. They staffed the Royal Council with middle-class lawyers, shifting power away from their aristocratic rivals. They sponsored explorations to the New World, including that of Columbus, reaping enormous rewards from the gold and silver discovered there. They also used wars—against the Muslims, the Jews, other Catholic kingdoms, and Protestants—to further consolidate their rule. By 1519, Ferdinand and Isabella's grandson, Charles V, was named Holy Roman Emperor. He would have dominion over much of Europe, including Spain, Germany, Italy, and the Netherlands. He also ruled most of the "New World." Not since Rome had so much power rested in the hands of a single person.

In France, wars provided a similar excuse for concentrating power. The Hundred Years War, fought between France and England, had required more money than any one feudal lord could afford. Charles VII, the king of France, devised an ingenious solution: he taxed the peasantry while paying the nobles to join the army. The nobility thus avoided a drain on their resources, but since they were now dependent on the king for their incomes, they could not effectively challenge his power. Charles' great-great-grandson, Francis I, was a peer of Charles V, and, like Charles, is considered one of the first "Renaissance Monarchs." In 1516, he signed the Concordat of Bologna with the Pope, giving him the right to appoint bishops in France. This shifted power away from the Church and, as with war, concentrated it in the monarchy. This consolidation of power is a classic mark of the early modern world.

In England, the process of consolidation was different but still effective. After the Hundred Years War, England enjoyed relative peace with the other nations of Europe. Because of this, prosperity increased, taxes were low, and the Tudor kings were popular. This enabled the kings to bypass Parliament (which was dominated by nobles) on important decisions. Tudor kings also enlisted middle-class officials as Justices of the Peace, securing their local support for Tudor rule. All of this contributed to national stability and to the increasing acceptance of the rule of English kings. The Tudor king Henry VIII was a peer of Charles V in Spain and Francis I in France. As with these other two rulers, he is considered one of the emergent "Renaissance Monarchs," producing a centralized national system that is one of the hallmarks of the modern world.

## Beginnings of Modern Science

In a limited sense, science began with the experimentation of Europe's artisans, mechanics, and natural philosophers: men of the Renaissance. The process of looking at the world as it actually was, through reason rather than dogma, was one of the most distinctive contributions of the Renaissance. It proved the essential ingredient to re-conceiving the way the world worked, much as

Renaissance philosophers had reconceived man's place in the world.

One of the first inventors of modern science was the Swiss physician, Paracelsus. Ancient Greek medical wisdom taught that disease was the result of an imbalance in "humors" in the human body. But in 1536, Paracelsus propounded the germ theory of disease and a related theory that focused on chemical imbalances in the blood. Paracelsus was vehemently opposed, especially by those still wedded to the ancient Greek teachings. But his theory proved much more effective in treating disease and it gradually came to replace the older teachings. In the process, it exposed the failings of the older teachings and the limitations of their blind reliance on ancient authority.

Another of the early inventors of science was the Belgian physician, Andreas Vesalius. Before Vesalius, the practice of medical anatomy depended on the teachings of Galen, a Greek physician who had only examined the bodies of animals, never humans. (To the Greeks, cutting up a human body—even a dead one—was sacrilege.) But in 1543, Vesalius published the first book of anatomy that relied on the actual dissection of human corpses for its understanding. This represented a huge change from the past. It placed direct observation ahead of dogma in the search for understanding the world. It furthered the overthrow of both Church doctrine and Aristotelianism—the belief in the teachings of Aristotle as the principal source of all knowledge.

Copernicus was undoubtedly the most revolutionary of the early scientists. For millennia, man had believed that the earth was the center of the universe. The senses make this almost inevitable: all of the heavenly bodies plainly appear to rotate around the earth. All of the authorities of the western world—the Bible, the Catholic Church, and Aristotle—taught this as well. But Copernicus spent 17 years studying all known facts and in 1543 concluded that it was the earth that revolved around the sun, not the other way around.  In the Catholic version of things, man had been created by God, in the image of God, and placed by God at the center of the universe. So, Copernicus' discovery completely upended both the Church's version of the cosmos, and of man's understanding of himself and his place in it. The "downsizing" of Man's role in the universe would echo for centuries and is probably not even fully played out still today.

## Religious Revolution

Even before Copernicus and the rise of science, a challenge to Church authority was taking place in religious affairs. In 1517, a Catholic priest in a small town in Germany accused the Catholic Church of being corrupt. It used its power, he said, to make money by selling "indulgences" to the rich in exchange for a promise that their sins would be forgiven on Judgment Day. Martin Luther "protested" this corruption by nailing his famous *Ninety-Five Theses* to the door of his local church in Wittenberg. In classic Renaissance fashion, Luther had not only challenged Church authority, he had done so on the basis of his reading of ancient documents, in this case, the Bible itself.

For example, Luther noted that five of the Church's Seven Sacraments appeared nowhere in the Bible. Rather, Luther said, they were nothing more than the creation of men, of earlier Church officials looking for ways to accumulate power to themselves by keeping parishioners in guilt and fear and in thrall to ritual. (He did accept the two sacraments that did appear in the New Testament, baptism and communion.) Luther went on to state that knowledge of God's will could be known only by a person's direct communion with God, and not through the intermediation of a priest or pope. This was another example of Renaissance thinking: the focus on the individual man.

But these teachings posed direct and profound challenges to the authority, even the legitimacy, of the Catholic Church. They were met with violent resistance from the Church itself, leading to a series of religious wars that wracked Europe for over a century. Luther's charges against the Church were quickly taken up by others, including John Calvin and Huldreich Zwingli. They, too, developed ardent followings that protested abuses of the Church and disputed its authority over secular affairs. These protests of Church abuses and the attempts at reform of the worst of Church practices became known as the Protestant Reformation. The movement proved unstoppable.

Protestantism was taken up by Henry VIII of England in 1535 to justify his second marriage when the Pope would not annul his first. It became one of the most powerful impetuses for the religious founding of America—the Pilgrims, Puritans, and Quakers who sought a place to practice their beliefs free from persecution in Catholic-dominated Europe.

## The Rise of Capitalism

Capitalism didn't spring up all at once. But its rise paralleled the Renaissance and accelerated in the years following. The causes were diverse but three particular changes stand out as critical: 1) changes in the status of labor; 2) the rise of a merchant middle class; and, 3) the widespread use of money as a store of value and a medium of exchange. These are among the defining traits of a capitalist system.

First, as noted above, the status of labor changed dramatically between 1450 and 1550. The Black Plague had killed 25 million people across Europe during the 1300s. Then, the Hundred Years War killed perhaps 5 million more. These losses made workers scarce and greatly improved the value of common laborers—the serfs that made up the backbone of feudalism. Feudal lords began having to compete for laborers to tend their fields and raise their livestock. Many resorted to paying money wages.

This marked the beginning of the end of the feudal system for it allowed workers to make a living outside of the traditional social contract of the landed feudal estate.

The second big change was the rise of a merchant middle class. After the fall of Rome, all economic activity became local and self-sufficient. Gradually, however, trade between regions grew. Those who managed this trade, merchants, held periodic fairs, which eventually became towns. These merchants had incomes independent of the landed feudal estates. This freed them from dependence on either the feudal nobility or the Church. These were the first true capitalists. In the cities of northern Italy the wealthiest of these merchants became the patrons of the Renaissance. The Medicis, Borgias, Sfortzas and other wealthy merchant families financed many of the period's greatest works of art.

The third big change ushering in the capitalist system was the growth of money as a widely accepted medium of exchange. Throughout the Middle Ages, most exchange was conducted by barter. But as trade expanded, goods could not be moved so easily. So, a more portable "store of value" had to be developed, one that could facilitate exchange of goods—but without the goods themselves! That, of course, was money. Then, after the discovery of the New World and its vast quantities of silver and gold, the supply of money exploded. This increased the status and power of the merchants who used, borrowed, and lent money for the goods they bought and sold. It also produced a European-wide inflation which hurt the nobility whose incomes came from rents that were typically fixed for life.

All of these changes—in labor, in merchants, and in money—conspired to alter the essential character of European life. Each of them had the effect of reducing the power of the traditional nobility while raising that of labor and the new, emerging middle class. They not only brought down one of the enduring foundations of the Middle Ages, feudalism, they put into play one of the most powerful and productive forces the world has ever known: Capitalism.

## Global Exploration

We don't usually think of it, but global exploration is one of the most dramatic events to emerge from the Renaissance. In the early 1400s, the Portuguese, under King Henry "The Navigator" learned how to sail ships into the wind by "tacking," or using the vacuum created when a sail is put at a diagonal to the wind. This made it possible to sail up and down the coast of Africa, or anywhere for that matter, and—even more important—reliably return. Such exploration was aided by recent improvements in navigational technology, including sextants (used to calculate latitude), compasses, and mechanical clocks. Then, when the Ottoman Turks captured Constantinople in 1453, European merchants were forced to look for an alternative route to India and its treasure trove of spices and silks.

This, of course, was the motivation behind Columbus' four epic journeys to America—or what he thought was India. In 1498, shortly after Columbus had reached America, Vasco de Gama, sailing for Portugal, rounded the Cape of Good Hope in southern-most Africa, and reached the real India. This produced huge riches from the spices he brought back and set off an explosion of exploration. In 1522, Ferdinand Magellan captained a fleet of Spanish ships that sailed around the world. By 1535, the Spanish conquistador Cortez had conquered Mexico and Pizarro had subdued Peru. In 1543, the Jesuit missionary Francis Xavier landed at Shimonoseki in Japan.

Thus, the center of European economic power shifted from the wealthy city-states of northern Italy which had monopolized the spice trade through Constantinople, to the Atlantic-facing states of Spain and Portugal. Soon, the center would shift again, to the larger and more dynamic Atlantic-facing states of France and England. European nations began setting up, first, trading outposts and later, diplomatic and military installations throughout the world. Within decades they would begin making colonies of many of these countries in order to extract their wealth and return it to the mother country.

This process culminated in the late nineteenth century with Europe and its descendant countries controlling more than 90% of the world. Of all the civilizations of the world, Europe alone, carried by the powerful new technologies developed during the Renaissance, dominated the seas and, therefore, the world.

# 6  Why Here? Why Now?

New concepts of man. New expressions in art, letters, and other media. Challenges to established authority. New institutions in economics, science, religion, and government. Changes of such magnitude would be revolutionary in any civilization. It is impossible, then, to view such an astounding array of events happening in so many areas and so closely together in space and time and not ask two obvious questions: 1) Why did they happen here, in Europe; and, 2) Why did they happen at this particular time? After all, other civilizations—India, China, and Islam—had deep, rich histories and thoughtful, dynamic people. But these civilizations produced nothing like the explosive transformation that happened in Europe. Why not?  Three explanations come to mind.

First, the existing order in Europe—the singular religious orthodoxy of the Catholic Church and the feudal system that had prevailed for a thousand years—had slowly but irretrievably begun to break down. The Crusades of the Middle Ages had killed many of Europe's nobility and liberated the serfs who fought in exchange for freedom on their return. The Black Plague of the 1300s was incomparably destructive, killing as much as half the population in some areas. Centuries of war (and especially the Hundred Years War) had also drained economic resources and strained social relations. The rise of commerce undermined traditional values and patterns of behavior. And the Catholic Church, which had harbored the flame of civilization through a thousand years of Darkness, had become arrogant, stagnant, bureaucratic, and corrupt. As all of these foundations of the old order crumbled, Europe became in need of, and almost perfectly poised to accept, something new.

Second, it was at precisely this time that that something new came along. At first it was Petrarch's rediscovery of ancient Rome. But that quickly expanded to include an equal reverence for rediscovered classical Greece. Through contact with the Islamic world, the writings of the ancient Greeks that had long been lost to the West were revived. They infused Europe with a new-found intellectual vitality, one that pre-dated the Catholic Church. It centered on man instead of the Christian God, and on reason instead of faith.

Then, when Constantinople fell, many of the world's Greek scholars fled to the wealthiest cities in western Europe, those of northern Italy. They brought with them not only the wisdom of

Greece but the instruments of the larger Orient as well. This included, from Islam, knowledge of astronomy, medicine, chemistry, mathematics, and navigation. And from China, technologies such as paper, gunpowder, moveable type, and the magnetic compass. All of these were superior to anything the West possessed at that time. This injection of new intellectual stimulus into a civilization perfectly poised to receive it resulted in the creative explosion we now know as the Renaissance.

Finally, and most importantly, the Renaissance was the first time that all three of the essential genetic roots of Western Civilization had come together at the same place and the same time. The oldest of these roots was the Faith of the Jews who had conceived of God as a singular, male human-like being. That faith continued in Christianity's concept of a man-god who had come to earth to absorb the sins of humanity. The second of these genetic roots was the Reason of Greece, recently returned from the Byzantines. The third and final genetic root was the Order of Rome, which had produced a vast physical infrastructure and an equally vast intellectual body of common law. These manifestations of Order had been maintained through the Church's administrative apparatus.

Faith, Reason, and Order came together in this place and at this time, to produce an explosive synthesis, unlike anything the world had ever known before. Faith was combined with the Greek reverence for the individual thinking man to produce Humanism, and artists of astounding creativity. Faith combined with Reason in the person of Luther to challenge authority in a way that neither Faith nor Reason could do alone. Reason combined with Order to allow insights into the workings of the natural world that would become science. And so on through a thousand episodes that confronted the existing world with the kind of confidence, optimism, and creativity that would be necessary to put that very world aside and birth a new one.

Faith, Reason, and Order—and more importantly, their combination—found their most felicitous expression in the arts that revealed man's highest understanding of himself. Inevitably, however, they came to be embodied in the larger cultural systems that ordered society: government, science, economics, religion, and technology. These organizing systems would prove more effective, more influential, more far-reaching, and more durable than art alone. They were reborn just as surely as artistic expression had been and they would apply themselves not just to rearranging the affairs of Europe, but to those of the rest of the world as well. They would propagate themselves to every civilization on earth, eventually changing the way all other civilizations understood themselves and the world.

# 7  Final Word

The Renaissance was one of the greatest example in history of the capacity of human imagination and will to dramatically reorder human affairs. Only such an imagination could compel a Petrarch to see man and not God as the measure of all things. Only such an extraordinary vision of man in the world could enable Michelangelo to see *David* in a block of marble and enable him to "liberate" the figure for all the world to see. Only such a combination of immensely powerful traits—Faith, Reason, and Order—could sustain a Copernicus for seventeen years until he could literally re-order the known universe. Only such a vastly improbable will could gird a Columbus or a Magellan to defy all convention, risk their own lives and those of their crews, to prove to the world that the world was round. Nothing less could empower a Luther to single-handedly shatter the religious unity which had held together an entire continent as a singular religious entity, Christendom, for over a thousand years.

The Renaissance had begun as a reawakened vision of man in the world, man measured not by the ethereal standards of a mystical, religious ideal but by the practical standards of man himself. But it soon outgrew its own origins in Rome and Greece. While it could not escape those essential cultural roots, it did re-order them in new and powerful ways that the world had never seen before. All of the amazing achievements of this pivotal century are in one way or another the result of the re-emergence and the interaction of these forces, in precisely this right place, at precisely this right time. No other civilization could have produced and propagated the new culture that Europe had, for no other civilization was experiencing the kind of systemic breakdowns that Europe was, and no other civilization had the genetic roots that Europe had in Israel, Greece, and Rome.

For good or for ill, within three hundred years all of the other civilizations on earth would come under the influence of European civilization. Science, Capitalism, and the Nation State would eventually come to be the organizing institutions not only of Western Civilization, but of almost all civilizations. Though it would take several more centuries for these forces to play themselves out, they were the unquestioned genesis of the modern world.

# 8 Timeline

1310    **Giotto's** *Deposition of Christ*

1341    **Petrarch**, Father of the Renaissance,
        named poet laureate of Florence

1422    **Ghiberti's** *Doors to the Florence Baptistry*

1427    **Masaccio's** *Holy Trinity*

1436    **Brunelleschi** completes the *Cathedral of
        Florence*

1438    **Donatello's** *St John the Evangelist*

1440    **Valla's** *Donation of Constantine*

1453    End of the Hundred Years War.

        Turkish cannons destroy Constantinople

1455    **Guttenberg** invents the printing press.

1480    **Boticelli's** *Primavera*

1485    **Alberti's** *De Re Aedificatoria*, the Bible of
        Renaissance architecture

| 1486 | **Mirandolla's** *Oration on the Dignity of Man* |
| 1492 | **Columbus** discovers the New World |
| 1500 | Since 1455, six million books have been printed in 40,000 different editions |
| 1504 | **Michelangelo's** *David* |
| 1505 | **Leonardo's** *Mona Lisa* |
| 1509 | **Erasmus'** *In Praise of Folly* |
| 1510 | **Raphael's** *School of Athens* |
| 1512 | **Michelangelo** completes the *ceiling of the Sistine Chapel* |
| 1513 | **Machiavelli's** *The Prince* |
| 1516 | **Thomas More's** *Utopia* |
| 1517 | **Martin Luther's** *Ninety-Five Theses* begins Protestant Reformation |
| 1522 | **Magellan's** crew completes first voyage around the world. |
| 1532 | **Cortez** of Spain conquers Mexico. |
| 1535 | **Henry VIII** of England quits the Catholic Church |
| | **Pizarro** conquers Peru |

1536     **Paracelsus** propounds germ theory of disease

         **Calvin's** *Institutes of the Christian Religion*

1543     **Copernicus'** *On the Revolution of the Celestial Spheres*

If you enjoyed this book, please look for all of the titles in The Best One-Hour History series.

- Ancient Greece
- Rome
- The Middle Ages
- The Renaissance
- The Protestant Reformation
- European Wars of Religion
- The English Civil Wars
- The Scientific Revolution
- The Enlightenment
- The American Revolution
- The French Revolution
- The Industrial Revolution
- Europe in the 1800s
- The American Civil War
- European Imperialism
- World War I
- The Interwar Years
- World War II
- The Cold War
- The Vietnam War

To learn more about each title and its expected publication date, visit: *http://onehourhistory.com*

# If you could change the world for a dollar, would you?

## Well, you CAN.
## *Now*, WILL you?

**One Dollar For Life**™ helps American students build schools in the developing world, for a dollar. *We can help you build one, too!*

Since 2007, we've built 15 schools and 23 infrastructure projects in countries like Nepal, Haiti, Nicaragua, Kenya, Malawi, and South Africa.

Haiti

Imagine if you and all of your school's students felt the pride of building a school so another child could go to school. Well, you can! For a dollar.

ODFL will help your club or school organize a fundraiser where *every dollar donated goes into a developing world project*.

Nepal

Make all of your school's students into heroes! It's easy, it's fun, and it's changing the world.

All profits from
*The Best One Hour History*™
series go to support ODFL.

Kenya

## You see, you *can* change the world.
## *Now*, WILL you?

Visit: odfl.org
**f** OneDollar ForLife
email: info@odfl.org   Phone: 661-203-8750

Made in the USA
San Bernardino, CA
23 September 2013